Your Best Gift Ever

*Embrace the Power of Life,
Become Who You Are and Get
What You Want*

Jay K. Morley

To You, Reader,

it´s the time to discover yourself

As a way of saying thanks for purchasing this book, there is a gift for you. A more topical issue than ever. Find out how to avoid falling into sneaky fear traps and stay healthy.

Simply copy and paste the link below into your browser, to get your gift:

https://dl.bookfunNEL.COM/61q2slgkvy

Table of Contents

Introduction

Realizing that you're unique is essential. It's about you and the things you can get and accomplish. Life has given you an incredible power as a woman, and becoming aware of it is fundamental.

Understanding who you are and discovering your true self, allows you to be complete, to become who you are, and to get what you want.

Many women ignore this aspect, unfortunately. They don't investigate their needs and desires; they don't study and don't pay attention to their peculiarities as unique human beings, of which each one is a world of its own, with its own merits and defects.

To live every day without knowing oneself, without getting to the bottom of one's personality, understanding one's characteristics leads to an existence that is not complete and deprived of the awareness of one's potential. And this implies as a result of not being able to seize the opportunities that life offers, and therefore not living it fully.

Sometimes women are afraid to "dig", to discover what lies beneath and reveal what they are. It also prevents an existence full of satisfaction.

This book is about understanding what separates you from knowing yourself well and discovering the gift you have. This gift represents what allows you to embrace the authentic power of life to become who you are and take what you want.

Often it is fear that prevents you from doing this—a sort of concern for the unknown, for what you can discover about yourself.

And the problem is that if you do not deepen your knowledge of yourself, that is, of your true self, you do not live fully because you do not know yourself thoroughly. In that sense, you don't know what makes you happy because you haven't lived it yet.

The values that matter may not be the ones that you have been taught, and based on which you have lived until now.

In this book, a great effort has been made to make it simple and understandable to everyone. It develops through a series of chapters, each of which goes to examine a criticality. They are the ones that prevent you from discovering who you are and your uniqueness, the extraordinary gift that you have carried with you since birth.

The pages that you are going to read, analyze, and explain the aspects that can help women like you to transform their lives, as well as the most common mistakes that prevent it.

Together, you will discover solutions to these obstacles in stages that are easy to complete.

Some of the common challenges that are faced are identity, self-confidence, family conditioning, setting high goals as the rule, lack of purpose, and dependence on the opinions of others.

In this book, you will learn to forge your uniqueness and make peace with who you are. It will allow you to stop limiting yourself to the professional and personal sphere.

You will also learn how to rely on your values rather than the opinions of others, and to resist the common, negative patterns in which women get involved.

You will become aware of your best gift ever: your uniqueness, with which you can embrace the incredible power of life and enjoy yourself.

There is a little you inside, waiting to blossom. This book will teach you how to find it, nourish it, and grow it to become the best you.

Chapter 1: Discover Yourself, You're Unique

Going in search of ourselves may seem vague, or sometimes silly, especially if we take it for granted that we already know us well, and there is nothing more to discover. It's hardly ever like that.

It happens when we are exactly sure that we have written a letter well and then, rereading it out of scrupulousness, realize that there are mistakes, that specific sentences should be changed, and so on.

Control and revision are what makes us aware of the path we still have to take.

You are the one who is with you 24 hours a day, seven days a week. You are the one who knows everything about yourself. You can't expect others to know. These are things that you have to take care of. However, as a busy woman, you may feel swallowed up by your professional and family obligations, losing sight of your real needs in the chaos of everyday life.

You probably forget to listen to your little inner self, who knows what you exactly need until that voice, still not paying attention to it, becomes surprisingly silent. She tried to warn you; now it's up to you.

This little self is often overlooked and pushed behind many things that you have to do for others, and others want you to do. And those are the cases where you find yourself wondering, "but for me, what am I doing?" Again, it's your little voice inside asking you.

Now it's time to get her out of the dark cage you've locked her in for too long, so you can do everything you never thought you could do. Offer yourself, because if you don't do it, nobody will, the best gift ever. Start with the qualities that make you unique as a woman and give yourself awareness, happiness, and realization of yourself.

Among these pages, you can find the inspiration to start your path of development and personal growth, which, in other words, means happiness and love, keeping those qualities that make you an extraordinary being.

For years, society has taught women to sacrifice themselves and put others first; in doing so, many have stopped doing the things that give them inner peace and self-awareness.
This last aspect is fundamental; without it, we cannot even begin. To solve a question or a problem, you must first be aware that you have it. And to do that, you need a change of perspective.
To be satisfied with oneself means reaching goals and solving discomfort, getting back in touch with the parts of yourself that make you unique.
The point is this: you are never satisfied enough when you solve problems or achieve certain goals. The main prerequisite to get what you want is to be good with yourself. That is, you have to be satisfied and grateful from the beginning, and not, dissatisfied and greedy. You should be grateful, like you already got what you want. That's the secret. It may sound like nonsense, but it's not.

One of the easiest ways to understand who you are is to write in a diary, take daily notes about how you feel. By recording these ideas, feelings, and emotions, you can better reflect on what makes you happy and what causes you stress, and sometimes, real "self-harm acts."

One of the best times to write in your diary is before you go to bed at night or wake up in the morning. In doing so, we give an outlet for fresher reflections than when you start the day, comparing them to the wiser ones in the twilight. Of course, the diary should not be done only in those moments; if you wish, you can write every time you're inspired.
When you need a break or feel overwhelmed, take a few moments to write in your diary, it will help you to tune into yourself, lowering the "background noise" of life around you.

It may be precisely those aspects in which women feel insecure that make them emerge. This dynamic can reinforce certain aspects of the character that are crucial to achieving a specific objective. The things that criticize you are the very things that make you unique.

For example, perhaps you feel that in meetings, you are "too bossy", something that many women hear about, while their male counterparts in the same situation are regarded as "assertive" or "good leaders".

In this case, then look deeply into what makes you "overbearing," and try to find the positive characteristics. You are probably well organized, good at keeping people's attention, concise in your speech, or maybe a combination of all these things.

If, on the contrary, you are too quiet in meetings, you could be a good listener, with excellent "absorption" skills of ideas and concepts. Regardless of personality traits, there are likely components that you can use as positive and to your advantage.

Take some time for yourself. Reading this book is an excellent start because it is essential to find something to reflect and grow in whatever way you like.

If you spend all your time trying to do things for others, your identity will be eclipsed, erased. As time goes on, it will be harder for you to find yourself, because you almost won't recognize yourself anymore. If you continue to do things every day that do not "belong" to you, that is, not in line with your being and your personality; you will reach a point that you will never find yourself again.

It's better to do things that relax, like reading, meditation, relaxing treatments, cooking, or going to the gym. And these are just some of the endless possibilities.

Don't be afraid to spend time alone; it's so that you can only find your "lost" identity again. Sometimes isolation and being alone with yourself are the only way to grow up and understand how far you've come in life. And from here, think about where you want to go, and what you want to do. It's a way to stop the world and reset your life for a new beginning.

Taking care of yourself will allow you to take better care of your loved ones, the people around you who need you, because you will do it on a new basis.

Another significant step you can take is to talk openly to the people you care about most. Involve them in the process of discovering the things that make you happy and fulfilled. Make sure that those who understand you, accompany you on this journey. This because before, talking about isolation and being alone with yourself, I did not mean that you should neglect the people you love. On the contrary, this would only make you feel even more lost.

The important thing is to select, even with ruthlessness. Never let other people around you say who you should be and what you should do, but let them support the person you are rediscovering that you are. Above all, they must share positively the new habits and new activities that you might choose to start.

Learning who you are doesn't happen overnight, it doesn't happen by accident, and it's not easy. However, beyond the premises outlined in this chapter, the following sections will give you more information on how to forge and use your sense of self in the various areas that commonly cause women to hesitate.

w to retake control of your life and have it entirely in your hands.

Chapter 2: Your Sense of Self and Your Purpose

Understanding who you are is crucial for your well-being and health. You don't get it right away; you need to work on it a little bit. You have to find out what your purpose on this earth is, that is, what you came here to do, is what undoubtedly realizes you as a human being.

Without it, you miss something, and you feel it, you realize it. And you miss so much happiness and self-confidence, as well as many opportunities.

Once you understand who you are and what your role is, you will be able to satisfy that little bit of you that is waiting to thrive inside you. In the chapters of this book, we will see in more detail how to do this.

Get a higher power. Get inspiration from something that you feel is bigger than you and that you can draw from. It's something that can teach you a lot.

It is understood as a higher power, a dominant force in your life, what makes you want to get out of bed in the morning and live. It's easy to find, more than you imagine. For example, if you love Nature, you might like to hear birds chirping in the morning, the sound of the wind in the trees, or walking on the beach.

Your higher power should not only suggest how to use your energy, but should also give you strength. And a lot of it.

Explore the wonders of this land, without going that far. Just look around, maybe when you happen to go to the park, and you are in the true solitude to appreciate the rustling, noises and scents of Nature.

Don't think too much about what your gears are grinding in your mind; they might take you out of the area. The mind in these things is treacherous. Imagine instead, that you're a little girl getting the birthday present you've been waiting for so long. Imagine jumping up and down with enthusiasm for this gift. What gift would that be now? What would make you so excited about life?

Whatever it is, it indeed expresses your passions, and therefore represents what you should focus on. It is another one of those reasons that gives you purpose.

Study the topics that interest you without worrying if they will help you make a career in your work. If you like philosophy, read it even if you do not use it directly in your daily life. Try to take fifteen minutes (or more) a day to learn something new or build on the knowledge you already have.

While you do this, remember the things that gave you joy as a child.

When you told yourself and convinced yourself that something was impossible for you, it was because you were only afraid to face it.

Sure, everyone feels lost when they're trying something new, but that doesn't mean they shouldn't try it. Studying unusual things will help you better identify what excites you.

Learn to be grateful for the good things you have. Take at least five minutes of your day to appreciate your higher power, what you feel you are living for.

Do it the way you feel most comfortable with. You can say a prayer of gratitude, or take a few moments outdoors to feel the warmth of the sun on your skin or listen to the wind blowing through your ears.

Even if you are having a bad day, find something small to be grateful for.

Chapter 3: The First Primary Conditioning Factor

The family and the education received inevitably have a substantial impact on behavior. Even those who had the best childhood can still have open wounds, because no family is perfect, just as no family is without pleasant memories.

Parents and siblings are the first source of social interactions, and usually instill morals and beliefs.

No matter your education or social status, family life is crucial to who you are, impacting your formative years.

However, although you can hardly erase the primary family conditioning, your sense of self must not be inextricably linked to your family's identity.

The way parents behave significantly influences their feelings about themselves. A family that uses many "loving touches" can lead children to feel safer and have higher self-esteem.

On the contrary, a family screaming and belittling a child, almost always creates less confidence in him or her. Low self-esteem makes it hard to believe what other people say, what they offer, and the opportunities that present themselves.

Moreover, children tend to copy the behavior of their parents, assimilating their example into adulthood.

Therefore, families influence their children's identity in an infinite number of ways, ranging from domestic to social and personal life. Growing up, one then enters the phase of rebellion.

Sometimes, unconsciously, you become like your parents, even when you rebel against their influence.

In this case, the values received through education in the family may have a significant influence on the vision of reality. We should take the values we admire in our family and develop our own values.

It would help if you did not lose yourself in the desires of what others want you to be. Do not let your parents, grandparents, siblings or any other family member stand in your way or influence you.

You can respect them without having to be like them. Give yourself some distance, if necessary, and think about what life would be like without the pressure of your family.

We must stop complacency, even when it comes to the people closest to us. It is a question of setting limits. There is always a boundary between what we are and what we want in life and what they are. Pleasing others does not bring anything good.

It would help if you had independence from the family, or you will never be anything more than the identity they have given you.

Maybe you had a rough childhood, or your family life was tough. Whatever your situation is, don't be the wounded child you once were. Consider that almost all of us were hurt as kids, no matter how good our parents were.

Now, however, you can decide for yourself, take steps for your good, and let the extreme elements and aspects of the past stand aside. You can say goodbye to them.

Chapter 4: Set High Standards for Yourself

In this chapter, we will deal with a critical topic and provide some useful advice for its success: the possibility of setting high-level objectives.

When you feel restless or unproductive, while trying to get your life back on track, break the patterns: start from a high standard. Feel ambitious, set goals, and stay focused on completing them.
When you do, you show that you can accept yourself and your real will to improve.
It also allows you to be more resistant to those who want to pressure you to act in other ways. If your standards are high, no one can tell you that you are not doing enough.

So how do you proceed?

The primary thing to do is to set a series of objectives. Don't just set one. Think of them as stepping stones tied to each other, leading you to a broader purpose.
Set plans across multiple areas of life and try to maintain them. There is no method or recipe for this; it is up to you to find the right goals for you. The important thing is that you feel this priority, and life will channel you towards them.

Reward yourself for a job well done whenever you reach a goal or make a positive change, don't be afraid to celebrate your success.
Keep pushing the things you want. Above all, don't structure goals just because you think they will be impressive for others. You don't need their approval, and ultimately, you don't need their support. Whatever you want to do, you can do it on your own.
Don't use social, mental schemes to determine if your goals are

high enough. Only you can determine what is essential to yourself.

Also, avoid comparisons. That is not a priority, and it leads nowhere. It just represents a bad habit that distances you from your goals, sometimes encouraging envy.

Trying to be a perfectionist doesn't help. You have to realize that you'll make mistakes, you'll miss goals, but that's perfectly normal.

High standards do not imply the absence of faults, because these serve to improve you, not to make you stop being yourself. Imperfections are part of you; recognize them, and accept them.

Chapter 5: The Quality of Your Life Is Up to You

Life can become difficult to manage when we make it uncontrollable.

It is normal to fear these circumstances, but it is not healthy to let this worry become an obsession, or cause an emotional upheaval, or fail to react.

You are always in control of your life, even when you feel that events and circumstances are doing so.

The only one responsible for how you react to a specific situation is you, and consequently also for everything that life offers you.

Controlling your life is sometimes not an easy task, but we can follow guidelines to do so. Use the following tools to make sure that you are always left with a certain quality even when you feel overwhelmed and find it hard to understand why everything keeps happening to you.

Again, take care of yourself. When life begins to slip out of control, the first thing people do is to neglect themselves, that is, not take care of themselves anymore.

This also has a psychological implication: you often feel almost useless when everything else seems so overwhelming.

It´s essential, in that case, to make sure your body and mind are taken care of as a basic principle, or you´ll start to notice cracks in all the other parts of life.

Taking care of yourself can be as easy as getting an adequate amount of sleep and water; two of our priority needs as human beings.

Let yourself be guided by what you feel inside, by your instinctive energy; the creative force that looks at you and calls you, can truly motivate you.

It is the key to all your reality. When you feel lost, you appeal to this "higher power" to find inspiration.

When you divert your attention from what you perceive as

your own, to pursue ambiguous paths away from your way of being, you go out of your "flow." Your life can then suffer setbacks and face unexpected obstacles.

You pursue your hobbies. Do it with all your might. Whatever it is, use your hobby to release and cultivate your creative energy.

Whenever you go through a period of difficulty, such as marital problems, grief, disappointment, and deep bitterness, do not overlook what makes your life go on and on smoothly. Do not lose the "compass", because afterward it becomes quite complicated to recover.

When things get complicated, pay more attention to taking care of your emotional and physical needs. Don't fall into the trap of blaming bad luck or fate for the circumstances you're in.

You alone are responsible even when you don't feel that way.

And you have the power to change situations; you have to learn to see them from a different perspective that most of the time, is not the one that you have been taught and that you have followed until now.

An essential psychological aspect is to surround yourself with people of value who can help you—having "support", having someone close to you can make the difference in overcoming an awkward moment.

Noise travels hand in hand with physical activity, as it increases endorphins, which are chemicals produced by the brain and classified as neurotransmitters. They go through your body, making you feel better.

Going to the gym is also a positive physical and social experience that has a significant influence on your mood.

But if you don't like the gym or don't have time to go to one, it works excellent to exercise at home with the equipment.

Beyond these possibilities, take a simple walk or dance in bed on the notes of your favorite songs. No matter what you do, move your body.

Chapter 6: Getting Self-Esteem and Self-Confidence

Believe it or not, trust and self-esteem are attainable by anyone with a certain amount of strength and the practice of self-reflection. Some people may need more effort than others, but with time and patience, results can be achieved, and trust can be truly cultivated.
But specifically, how do we do it?
First of all, remember what makes you unique, and never forget that you have a purpose.

Let's start with consideration of yourself, which is the most critical aspect. We must eliminate negative self-esteem. All those limiting thoughts and behaviors such as *"I'm too fat"*, *"It's not for me"*, *"I can't do it"*, *"Everyone will hate me"*.
They are all examples of things that many women say about themselves every day. Now, the right tactic to intervene effectively is to observe yourself from the outside, that is, to become aware of when you're about to think or say something like that.
When you get caught saying one of these negative things, replace it with something positive and uplifting. *"I love the way my clothes show off my colorful personality"*, *"I'm smart even if I make mistakes"*, or *"Lots of people still love me"*.
The exchange of thoughts, from negative to positive, can completely change your mood and the way you feel about yourself.

Now let's talk about the physical. It's hard for many women to say beautiful things about themselves, but that's a significant boost to self-esteem. You have to do it even when it feels forced or out of place.
Standing in front of the mirror, smiling, and looking at yourself can help create self-esteem. The more we laugh at ourselves, the more we begin to like ourselves.

Recognize all the things you love about the person you see in front of you in the mirror, but don't just look at your body, think about the beautiful things your body can do. Of course, your eye will inevitably fall on the defects, on what you don't like about yourself, but accept them and see them from a new point of view.

Let's explain it better. You don't have to try to love your flaws; if you don't like them, there's little you can do. But try to consider what you think are your flaws from another perspective. That's the secret.

Maybe you have stretch marks on your stomach from giving birth. Instead of hating them, observe them and repeat to yourself: "Wow, my body was able to give birth to a baby; this is incredible!". Erase the idea that there is something intrinsically wrong with you, and focus instead on the things your body and mind have allowed you to do. Whether your body has been used to procreate or to overcome a sports business, it represents something of absolute value. Also, be thankful for it, because it accompanies you every day, allowing you to walk, breathe, see, feel. Do not take all these things for granted. Don't make this mistake, and on the contrary, thank him for what he does for you.

Think about what you hate saying and question your self-criticism. It hasn't helped you much until now; it's only contributed to making you feel worse. It hasn't solved any problems for you.

If you're still not convinced, list all the things you don't like, but then ask yourself why you feel this way. While you're doing that, think of yourself as a child. Imagine telling that child all the bad things you usually say about yourself. Using that language on your childish self becomes incredibly tricky, so you shouldn't even use it on your adult self.

Imagine the scenarios or situations in which you feel most lacking in self-confidence. Imagine yourself at work, in your family, with colleagues or friends.

Are your insecurities intellectual, physical? Identify where

they are deepest and aim precisely at those areas. Ignoring your uncertainties won't help you eliminate them. So face them, bring them to light, and make yourself aware that they have no reason to exist.
You are not your faults, and your failures do not erase your worth.

Many women suffer from imposter syndrome, which is the tendency to think they are not good enough for the positions they hold and the responsibilities they have.
They feel like they're faking their credentials, even though they're as qualified as anyone else. This syndrome makes these people think that they are judged as impostors by their colleagues or friends, and they never feel that what they do is good enough to deserve the things they get out of life.
To combat this type of disorder, you have to start rebuilding your reputation for yourself in insecure areas.
The first things that generally have a significant impact on self-esteem are the failures. Especially when others remind us, colleagues or bosses, it is precisely here that we absolutely must not think of them as failures, but consider them as opportunities for growth.
Learning from what you have done wrong means improving, and objectives are achieved when you do not give up. Failure is an excellent motivation for those who want to emerge.

If you have a painful past, face it. Dig it out, observe it, find someone to talk to about it. Writing about those experiences helps a lot; it's a courageous and effective gesture to resolve such situations.
Unresolved problems and unmanaged traumas can hijack your ability to manage yourself properly to have a healthy life. Fighting against feelings of inferiority, shame, guilt, or even self-hatred is what makes it challenging to love yourself in the way you deserve.

It's important to recognize when you've done an excellent job, and accept its praise. In the diary, make a list of your achievements, it will help you to "applaud" and feel "promoted". Feeling proud of your professional success, and expressing your happiness does not make you arrogant at all. Share and celebrate your achievements with those you love the most.

Chapter 7: Accept the Fact that Not Everyone Can Accept You

Even if you learn to accept yourself, which you absolutely must do, you must also learn to admit that not everyone can do the same with you.

A solid self-esteem is not affected by the fact that others can't appreciate us. It has to be taken into account as a natural aspect and part of ordinary reality.

Beyond what you think, whether it's right or not, rejection must never destroy the image you have of yourself.

Accepting this situation allows you to be yourself and not to worry about people's judgments about what you do and what you say.

The fact that certain people don't like you doesn't make you a wrong person at all. You don't have to pay attention to this aspect and make it a personal matter, or a matter of principle. It is part of life and social relationships.

Saying *"You are so wrong"*, *"You are badly dressed"*, or *"You are so bad at it"* does not change you as a person. You're not the mistakes you've made. You're not the failures you've suffered.

What people say contrary about you doesn't define you the same way that what they tell you are doesn't determine you.

Don't take criticism personally, because sometimes people can say cruel things about their insecurities more than you.

Even if that's the case, you are the same as when you woke up that morning, and as long as you do your best to be the right and happy person you want to be, that's enough.

No one can steal your achievements and your uniqueness.

It can sometimes happen that the people who do not accept you are the ones whose opinions are most important to you. Parents' views, for example, are usually valuable, which does not mean that they are correct at all. However, sometimes parents and other family members, friends or loved ones, do not accept certain things about you. It could be your sexuality, your weight, or perhaps the way you raise your children. Whatever they cannot take, their rejection will probably be painful for you.

However, you cannot be someone else to please the people you love, because you would not be true to yourself. You would repress the essential parts of yourself that make you unique.

So you're wondering, do I have to cut ties with people who don't accept me?

Let's say that sometimes a "diplomatic" isolation can make sense, especially when you're in the starting phase of a life or professional project, which could prove to be "critical" to your loved ones. It is best to "re-emerge" afterward, when a project or action has been carried out. Whether it is a success or not, no one can say anything.

Finding safe and consolidated spaces where you can be yourself is very important. Clubs, associations, and online forums are great options for finding people who share the same interests as you. They make you feel that you are not alone in a particular situation, and the opinions and criticisms of others, perhaps parents or close relatives, really take second place, losing importance and "deflating".

When overcoming the opinions of others becomes complicated; most of the time, this is related to your profound insecurities. So try to become aware of why certain things affect you so deeply to understand what is the key to overcoming insecurities.

It is fundamental to teach yourself, through practice, to resist the offense of the disapproval of others. The fact that others do not like you or that they disapprove of your choices is a problem that does not affect you.

When everything seems to go wrong, remind yourself of what makes you unique. Review the things that make you feel safe. Don't let the wrong or sad thoughts occupy your mind. They only cause unnecessary pain and suffering, monopolizing the mental energy you could use for constructive purposes.

Feeling undue pressure within yourself to try to live up to the expectations of others, or to please them, is the most wrong and misleading for your happiness and your person. Accept yourself as you are, no matter what others would like you to be.

Chapter 8: What People Think. Let's Think Different

Human beings are sometimes self-harm creatures, so millions of people make the same excuses day after day, year after year. People continuously fall into certain common mental traps as they try to achieve their goals.
It is essential to demystify these pranks to show how one can change the way of thinking and achieve goals that are considered impossible.

One of the worst things that can be said is, "I can't." The moment you say these words, you declare to yourself that what you want to do is impossible.
The thinking and the possibilities close in. You stop grasping the alternatives, and you assume that you will not succeed. If the Wright brothers, heroes of aviation, had taken it for granted that human beings could never fly, we would certainly not know their names today.

Try recording in a diary every time you say, maybe almost without realizing it, that you can't do something. You might be surprised how many times you say it. But above all, don't assume you can't do it just because you're afraid of failing or getting a "no".
An annoying phrase is, "I couldn't do it anyway". Stop here. Don't try to predict the future. You don't know at all that you're going to fail.
This sentence comes out of a cliché made of fear and, of course, that's what many people have thought at some point in their lives.
However, it is something that you have to fight hard, especially at the beginning. Resist the impulse to take failure as a rule, or even just as a possibility, and start thinking about success instead. Start telling yourself that whatever you want to achieve, you can do and succeed.

Of course, success is not guaranteed, because it's all in your hands, but make sure you take the risk that the only real failure may be to give up trying and do nothing.

Sometimes, when you're a bit older, you start saying something like: "It's too late."

When you think something like that, you are the victim of another limiting mental scheme that you have imposed on yourself. And in fact, it is what you will miss out on to be successful and succeed in the business.

It's not too late for me to do something. There are examples of people in their seventies and even more who have founded companies, put themselves back in the game, and won. People in their nineties who continue to train and play sports. Of course, there are not many of them, but they are precisely the ones who have never thought "It's too late", because everyone else thinks so, and they don't do such enterprises. That's why almost 99% of people fail.

You can go back to senior college, if you have the means, no matter how long you've been away from academia. You can start giving or taking piano lessons as a 70-year-old, if that's what gives you satisfaction.

In our culture, older men are called "distinguished," while older women are told they look suitable for their age.

It makes it seem like the best years have passed, but as long as you are still alive, you can face new challenges and try new experiences that you may have been waiting for all your life. And maybe that's what will make you live longer.

The last common excuse people use not to do things is that they don't have enough time. It's true that you only have twenty-four hours in a day, but the point is that time is limited, and that's an indisputable truth. Apart from all the techniques to improve your day's organization, when I say that I don't have time, I enter a sort of time loop so I'll have less time to do things. In this sense, it is I who narrow it down myself—another excuse customarily used to avoid acting.

Priorities need to be set, but if you stop watching TV for just one hour a day, or give up chatting on social media with acquaintances, you might have several extra hours a week to do more productive things.

Now, making excuses for things you're afraid to do is normal. But recognizing and admitting that these fears separate you from your goal is a big step towards achieving it.

Chapter 9: What People Do. Let's Do Otherwise

If you feel lost, restless or dissatisfied with life, due to specific circumstances or situations, you are not alone. Millions of people experience similar conditions - life going off course.
Most of these people don't know how to get back on track. Sound familiar?
If it does, don't worry about it. What unhappy or dissatisfied people do and say, they reveal a lot about what you absolutely should not do.
Seven are the main problems that hinder people's success. Reading the list, you may find that one or more of these points apply to you as well.
Learn the mistakes that others commonly make and then do the opposite.

One of the most common problems that hinder people's success is procrastination. Everyone does it, often, or even all the time. You say you will take care of a task later and keep telling yourself that until you never do. Procrastinating is dangerous because it puts pressure on you, condensing the amount of time you have to complete a task, and making it harder to produce quality work.
But procrastinating becomes mentally draining because the more you put it off, the more you worry about dealing with things. You postpone because you are afraid of failing, of not completing an assignment, or because it has to do with something "uncomfortable."
Procrastination is often confused with laziness. The two things are related, of course, but not necessarily. You can procrastinate out of laziness, but most of the time, it's out of insecurity.

The good news is that you can improve insecurity, and while

you work on your confidence, there are immediate steps you can take to avoid procrastination.

Start by dividing the tasks into manageable parts. Large projects may seem cumbersome and impossible to complete, but if you break them into sections and subsections, and tackle them one at a time by focusing on it, you will feel less overwhelmed.

Set goals to complete these individual pieces, and write them down. Research shows that you are more likely to accomplish the goal when you compile a list of things to do.

Also, always remind yourself that you can do the work you are doing correctly and effortlessly. Repeat it to yourself several times.

Finally, keep in mind that the work may not be perfect. There may be mistakes, and changes may be necessary, but this is not abnormal or shameful. It just means that you still have to learn.

A second common mistake of people is resisting change. Of course, leaving something for something else is difficult; it requires strength, will, motivation. Sometimes it's done out of desperation, and this is when it's easier to do so.

Those who have changed so often in life know what we're talking about: it's the feeling of running to keep up with something that we don't fully understand yet, and we're not in control of at all. It is the dynamic, whether we change by choice or we do so because circumstances force us.

When things evolve, we begin to understand that this was a good thing. Without change, life would be quite dull, and we would sometimes miss the best opportunities.

Change is about embracing, not fighting. Doing the opposite would make everything vain.

But let's practice and try to make changes even small, almost invisible, but every day. Maybe we vary part of our daily routine, to test how versatile we can be with ourselves and with life. We don't have to prove anything to ourselves, just experiment.

In this way, when life confronts us with a change, even a traumatic one, we will be "trained", and it will seem less demanding and more comfortable to deal with.

On the contrary, resistance to change leads us to fight against the inevitable and sometimes the imponderable, what we do not yet know. It becomes an "invisible enemy" that we have to face by force, but with few weapons, and the will is not enough. Better to make friends with change, and accept it as part of the rules of that game called Life.

If you think it's just lovely words that are difficult to put into practice, there's no other way to manage it, only with practice and habit. That's why it's important not to do the same things every day, of course, I'm referring to free time, which depends on us and in which we have free will.

Through change, we have the power to improve ourselves.

I have repeated it several times in these pages. Please don't please others. It is a practice that empties you and deprives you of the energy necessary to concentrate on your things.

You've learned that people won't always accept you, so pleasing others doesn't make sense anymore. Nor try to do it with the ones you love.

Start from the assumption that people accept you for who you are, especially with your flaws. One mistake to avoid is not to confuse complacency with making others happy; these are two very different things. Making others happy can be very satisfying, but this is not the goal. The satisfaction we get from it is only a consequence, a pleasant side effect.

You don't have to hide who you are to be loved and respected by others. If you try to please someone, you are just another person who suffocates their uniqueness, and these individuals go nowhere.

Many women doubt themselves. They think there's something wrong or out of place in what they want to do. They start projects and dream big ideas, but they don't finish them because, within them, they doubt if they can accomplish them. Believing they can do something, is what develops magic, the fluid that leads to seeing the final result.

But some people don't even reach the stage of doubt. They don't try; they don't even start. They refuse to let their dreams take them away.

Most failures originate from renunciation or fear. Of course, some dreams don't work. For some reason, you won't be able to realize them or even undertake them, but nothing prevents you, and this constitutes most scenarios, from taking parts of that dream and modifying them. If you can't achieve a goal, it means it wasn't for you. But don't preclude yourself from taking other paths. Do the opposite of what everyone else is doing, and you will succeed. Sure, maybe different from what you expected, but you'll have changed something in your life anyway.

Chapter 10: The Game of Perspectives. How You See Reality

Consider this. The way you see the world is not as it is, and it does not even align with the way others see it. Consequently, it can be challenging to understand the point of view of others and certain particular situations that seem "strange" to us. It is something that few of us are accustomed to judge by our yardstick. We're used to not looking only at one side of a building, when there are four. It changes perspectives. Not on the significant issues of life, but starting with the small everyday things. Don't judge, never.

When you feel actively involved in something, contemplate with detachment how other people see the same situation in a completely different way. Accept the different views of others, their points of view, and then let them go.
It would help if you did not change your opinion, nor should you force others to change theirs.
Practice empathy. Put yourself in the shoes of others, and understand that each person has unique experiences and difficulties. Do not belittle anyone who has an opinion different from yours. Such views are no better or worse than yours.

Listen actively, letting people talk about their perspectives. Do not take for granted what others want to say. Let them talk.
Seize the nuances of their words, and if something is not clear, ask questions to better understand, but I repeat, do not judge. You don't have to agree with them, but put aside hostility.

Now let's go and demolish your mental paradigms for a moment.
No perspective represents reality because reality does not exist. I am not referring to the material existence of things and objects, but to the way you see and consider the world.
No vision of reality can be considered "real". Everything boils

down to one question: what you think and how you think it is. Most of what you think of the judgments that you express thoughts and things that you think you know, you don't know them fully, or even they are entirely foreign to you. Not everything that you believe is true is right. Not everything is as it appears to you.

So what do you have to do? You're going to tell me that this way, you don't have certainty anymore.

That's right. Use all the information you can to get as much perspective as you can. Don't exclude specific ideas just because you don't like them, or don't make you comfortable.

When you get angry about something, lean on the reason for disappointment, on what discourages you, and embrace this unfriendly and challenging territory. This is what allows you to grow up.

Chapter 11: Your New Habit: Don't Judge, Never

The adage "don't judge a book by its cover" is more accurate than ever. Judging is often a way to unload frustrations almost having fun, and relegates us to the narrowest of views. It's like gossip. It's free nothingness in a vacuum.

People want to believe that their instinctive reactions towards others are correct, but such instincts are based on false foundations, such as race or sexual orientation.

The stigmas and judgments that permeate society, in general, are unconsciously used by people to make assessments of merit. So start from this assumption: judging is not suitable for your health, it hurts you more.

Judging others is the presumption of feeling superior. It's the false conviction that "it wouldn't happen to me".

The things you find hateful about others represent the aspects that frustrate you the most about yourself. And in doing so, you only draw attention to these negative qualities and continually strengthen them.

To judge others is to judge ourselves. Criticism of others opens the door to personal frustration and dissatisfaction.

Moreover, judgment invites confrontation, and this can make you feel insecure. It will not make you feel better, nor will it improve your situation.

When you judge other people, you close your doors. You raise the walls; you become rigid and resistant to any information that can refute our judgment. As a result, we create nothing good, and we become blind to the prospects that may present themselves.

Another good rule is not to jump to conclusions about people. Almost always, we do not know their situation and what they are going through. When you see a person begging, you don't see how they got to that point, and judging them will not help improve the situation.

I mean, look for the good in people, not the bad. You don't have to make an effort to give compliments when it's unnecessary, and in any case, you always have to go easy on compliments. You risk being mistaken for people who are not sincere, especially when you exaggerate. Let's say that it would be a good rule not to do them.

Instead, give birth to ideas that deserve compassion and respect, and that makes you experience those dimensions. Both are fundamental aspects of life, which contribute to making you feel better. They have an almost therapeutic effect; they heal the lousy mood by projecting you on a plane of well- being with yourself.

Each of us would not want to be judged by others. Even when we know we're not okay, maybe disheveled or tired early in the morning, we'd like to go unnoticed, almost "invisible".

But what's most important is not to judge yourself, because it means diminishing yourself. Everyone has wrong moments, in which we don't want to care about our appearance, and sincerely we don't care what other people think about us. We have to accept these moments and live them. We know that we are more than we appear, and those who appreciate us know that very well.

So let's avoid judgment; it's our enemy, and we have to treat it as such.

Chapter 12: How to Manage Unpleasant Feelings

It's not easy to feel happy all the time. Instead, you can be sad, angry, stressed, heartbroken, and feel a myriad of other negative emotions. It's a common fact, it happens, and it's part of our existence.

Sometimes it isn't easy to understand what you are feeling. Maybe you feel a sense of dissatisfaction without being able to understand what it's due to.

Emotions can get confused with each other, and consequently confuse us too. It becomes crucial to understand what's underneath, so that we can face the problem correctly and find the solution.

Always try to determine why you feel an emotion, whatever it is. Do not be afraid to dig and what you can find out.

There is no other way to understand what lies deep beneath the most superficial feelings. What you may be worried about may not be the real reason for your discomfort.

For example, you may collapse when your boss tells you that you have made a small mistake, but this is only the last drop of a specific situation that lasts.

The important thing is not to refuse and not to fight these feelings. If you try to do it, you get the opposite effect: they almost always get more potent, emptying you of energy. In a real sense, they "vampire" you.

Instead, you have to accept them, make yourself aware that they are there, and that you are living them, preventing them from taking the best of you and disrupting your days, if not even your life.

It puts you in a position to find positive strategies to face, solve the problem, overcome the worst circumstances, and stay with your identity intact.

Do not try to push away or counteract uncomfortable emotions, because, in this way, you feed them. What you need is the right clarity to deal with them.

If you ignore them, they will swell up to explode and then drag you into despair.

If you feed it, you will live badly because the problem and anxiety will get bigger.

The best strategy is to admit its existence and make yourself aware that you cannot suppress it, but solve it. In essence, you "rationalize" it by understanding its root, and this point, you dematerialize it.

Let's go back to the concept: if you ignore an unpleasant feeling or emotion, it's no use, because it's magnified; if feeding it is of no use, because I play its game, it's not even worth contrasting it.

The only way is to accept it, because it gives me the necessary clarity to understand its real reason, its original root. By doing this, the negative feeling loses strength to the point that it no longer has the motive to exist.

Chapter 13: Push What You Think Are Your Limits

In this chapter, we talk about limits. Knowing one's own, means making the difference between success and failure, between reaching a goal and not reaching it.

But knowing one's own limits can sometimes be problematic, not because it is objectively complicated, but because we, like most people, think we have already reached them or know them already. Well, it's not like that at all.

It is a mistake, a clear example of limiting conviction.

If you've reached a "peak", a success, or an essential goal in any field of your life, you feel as if you've reached your limits, as if you have nothing left to give and nothing left to do.

Now, put that idea aside, because what you think are your limits are just the beginning of something bigger. We've probably already heard that the only limits we have are the ones we impose on ourselves, which is equivalent to saying that we're used to sabotaging ourselves all the time.

We are led to think that others are always better than us or have better luck, especially when they succeed where we fail, and where we do not even allow ourselves to compete.

In the collective imagination, whoever succeeds in an enterprise, whatever it is, has challenged its physical and mental limits and emerged victorious.

Out of prudence, or instinct of self-preservation, we are inclined not to challenge ourselves, not to question ourselves, if not rarely.

Sometimes it's a matter of mere routine. We are creatures of habit who tend to do the same things every day, at the same time and in the same way. It is also a good thing, because routine helps us to be more productive, but too much method and rigidity can clip our wings, extinguishing our creativity.

Discovering what your limits are means expanding your horizons and being able to think in a new way. We need curiosity about ourselves. But first of all, you need the will to want to do it. It is also an excellent opportunity to face one's fears, because it is often precisely these that prevent us from grasping and accepting all that the world has to offer.

There is no law or rule, and the threshold of one's limits changes according to the situation and the moment. It varies according to our motivation, above all. Those who have already experienced them once could reach new ones in a completely different circumstance.

Discovering one's own "boundaries" implies not being content, not sitting on one's little successes, or continuing to cry over one's failures. One can fail several times before achieving success.

If you think "I am happy enough, I have arrived", you are undoubtedly settling for it. The exact situation that prevents you from being fully satisfied, discovering what your limits are. Living in gratitude for what you have does not exclude you from aiming for more, on the contrary, it constitutes the right substratum.

The word "content" is wrong, the phrase "thank you for what I have in life, and from here, I will have even more" is the right mindset.

Sometimes you let your imagination run wild, it's right for you. It should be one of your closest friends. Please do not push your dreams away because they seem silly or implausible to you. Embrace them and let them take their course because the only risk you have is to stumble into something magnificent. It never hurts anyone to imagine. Find the imagination of when you were a child, the same one that gave you hours and hours of fun. Find it again, keep it, and channel it into what you do for your goals.

Now and then, you have to challenge what you think is right because it could be linked to some limiting mental paradigm. Look for the controversy in the arguments, try to find out if the opposite of what you thought could perhaps open your eyes to situations or opportunities.

Doubt about beliefs and suppositions, search if there are flaws in them. Concerning trust, always keep the benefit of the doubt. Doubt forces us to think critically, learning more about the topics that interest us. Never stop challenging the world around you and the knowledge you have ascertained, because you cannot improve yourself if you think you already know everything.

Don't be afraid to change, because this is how you overcome your limits. Awaken that part of yourself that hasn't been out for a long time, that is locked in its comfort zone and refuses confrontation. You will get more when you recognize that you are more than you think and that you can do more than you imagine. There are no slopes that you can't overcome.

Chapter 14: Learn Your Lessons and Live By Your Values

The premises. In life, it is not always possible to make ideal decisions for yourself. Besides, not everyone can deal with the unexpected, all the more if it leads to upheavals in life.
Of course, one learns from mistakes, although sometimes at a considerable cost. So here is the concept of introducing one's values.

They define who you are, influencing the decisions you make. If you're confused about them and don't know what they are, you'll have a hard time figuring out which direction to go in. Fortunately, this rarely happens.
Our values are our GPS. They don't tell us which destination to go to, but they tell us which roads to take to get there.
Sometimes, we make bad choices, but as long as we hold on to what we believe in, we can learn from our mistakes and get back on track.

How do we determine your values? A good start is to write down what we believe in deep in our hearts, thinking about all the things we feel unshakable, that is, the fixed points of our lives.
They can be moral or ethical aspects, like treating people with respect or honoring parents, but they can also be more specific and refer to what I call the "higher power," our absolute belief. Each of us has it, and women more than men. Women are also more attached to it.
From the list of things you believe in, choose your ten fundamental values, the most important and intrinsic to what you are- those that guide you in your daily and life decisions.

Beyond the supreme values you believe in, what are the most critical areas of your life? Write the things that give you the most happiness and signal as values. Use them in social interactions and make more use of them. But also think about other areas of your life and take note of your values. You could learn more about yourself.

Let your mistakes guide you; they are inevitable. Accept them. You're not perfect, and you don't have to be. Even people with the highest and most reliable value systems do not have enough knowledge to apply their excellence to all situations correctly.
Mistakes are nothing but opportunities to do better next time. Don't be too hard on yourself.
Strengthen these beliefs by maintaining your moral faith even in the most challenging situations.
In any case, forgive the moments when you have not kept faith with your values. But when things get complicated, lean on them without hesitation so that they are your support.

Chapter 15: Think and Live at High Vibrations

Being able to think and live with high vibrations undoubtedly improves the quality of life. Keeping the vibrational frequency high means focusing on the things around you that stimulate your energy and inner peace.

Vibrations are the sum of your life's energies. The challenge is to be able to keep them high so that problems seem less annoying, and you can achieve your goals. If the vibrations are high, you will feel ready to start the day with new energy.

Try to eat well. The food you introduce into your body has a real impact on how you feel. Find healthy, energized foods. Fruits, vegetables, and whole grains can sustain you for a long time, while sweets and starches usually lead to an energy collapse.

That doesn't mean you can never indulge in candy and chocolate because they can make you feel good if eaten sparingly. But make sure you give your body the nutrients and energy it needs. Enjoy your food, but make sure you eat so that your body gets stronger.

But the most important thing for our body is to be well-rested, which means sleeping well. It's vital not to interrupt the sleep, because it gives the body the possibility to heal and recharge, finding new energy and motivation in the morning.

Even from the point of rest, people are not all the same. Some are used to going to bed late because they are more concentrated and productive in the evening, and those who like to get up at dawn and get active right away.

The best sleep is achieved during the first few hours, so going to bed early is more effective than getting up late in the morning. However, it is also essential to rest through moments of contemplation and relaxation to relax your mind. Studies have shown that meditation is beneficial in recharging the body's physical and mental energies. Forty minutes of meditation, so not even one hour, is equivalent in terms of rest to about three hours of sleep.

Another activity in which you can surely invest in is free time. If you're just back from a long and tiring day at work, do something that makes you feel good before you start doing chores. Free time is one of the most neglected human needs, but man struggles to stay productive and find inspiration without it.

Appreciate Nature. It has a high energy that can lift you and give peace to your mind. Breathe the air, enjoy and admire the beautiful creatures, plants, and wonders that Nature offers. Stop to perceive the scents of Nature, such as flowers and grass. They are a great way to get in tune with your senses and keep the vibrations high.

Dominate the worries that oppress you. We all have anxieties for various reasons, but not for this reason we must let fear affect our lives.
We can't make problems go away with a snap of our fingers, but we don't let the things or situations that worry us lower your vibrations. Let's keep the energy high, accepting stuff over which we have no control as characteristic elements of life.
Important: if you don't want to have sorrows, fighting against something invincible, accept to manage whatever life puts over your head. Denying or ignoring facts or situations is useless. Accept, because you are the only one responsible for the quality of life. I still remember: to accept does not mean to remain passive and do nothing, waiting for something or someone to solve things for us. Instead, it means to do something positive to find a solution free from fear and anxiety. It is the only way to find it.

Build love, compassion, and forgiveness, and try to live on this kind of vibration. Bring these elements into your everyday life, and make their dimension your own. It is beyond sorrows, disappointments, and anger.

Learn the problematic art of forgiveness - you need a lot of practice to succeed in it. Do not let the people who have hurt you come back into your life.

Maintaining high vibrations lifts your spirit, bringing you closer to the things that mean the most to you. This, by the way, is also the best way to find solutions to the problems that arise. It is not with negativity that you can solve certain complications of life.

Therefore, take some time to take care of all the activities that create positivity and positive energy.

Chapter 16: The Courage to Be Yourself

Sometimes it´s even harder for a woman. The world and society affect you. Finding the strength to be yourself may not be as easy as it seems.

The most excellent advice is to have the courage to be yourself in everything you do. You can find this strength only in yourself; you can't rely on anyone, and nothing else. There are no magic formulas.

Don't be afraid to remove the things you feel don't belong to you; maybe behaviors absorbed by other people or past experiences. Sometimes we say something or behave as if we weren't talking; these are the blatant effects of attitudes that we have absorbed from people close to us, friends, or relatives. Accept instead the good facets of your character that make you genuine and authentic. Also, don't be afraid of yourself and discover how you are. If it is about questioning what you know about yourself, do it without delay. It's always better to know the truth, and let it come out.

Digging and discovering who you are is not always easy and can reveal surprises, but don't let anything get in the way of your authenticity. You may find that you are a little different from what you always thought you were, and you have to accept it in this case.

When you begin to see parts of yourself that you have never noticed before, accept them, even if with discomfort or amazement. You still need them to lead a fulfilling life; you cannot deny them.

In other cases, you may even realize that you are almost a stranger to yourself, and maybe you no longer recognize yourself. Instead, be excited to meet this new person rather than afraid. It's your unique self. You could be a modern woman, and your life could change in ways you never expected.

When there are changes, because maybe you've become more

aware of something or yourself, don't let those around you put pressure on you.

Do not let the people you love, the people you admire, or the people you envy impose you as you present yourself to the world. It is emotionally mature to listen to others' opinions and recognize their desires, but you do not need to be them to understand them. You can see another person's point of view and appreciate it without losing yours. Adapting to the crowd is easy, because you don't take risks, but if you let others pressure you, you'll collapse your self-esteem.

Likewise, don't delude yourself that you're something you're not. Women often have a vision of how to behave, look and identify themselves. Many of these ideas come from social standards, criteria that are sometimes impossible to meet because they are too far away from what you are.

Remove the image of the perfect woman from your mind, if you ever had one. You don't have to be sure of something to be valuable. Assume that you already have value for who you are. And no one can take that away from you.

On the other hand, you can't feel confident if you wear someone else's face as a mask.

To get in touch with yourself, with your true self, start focusing on activities that can connect you to your uniqueness. Please take into account what you like to do and dedicate yourself to it in your free time. Cultivate your hobbies and passions, and give vent to your creativity. You don't have to want to look like someone else; you're unique.

Don't be ashamed of what you like and don't hide it. You don't have to justify anything to anyone. If you have hobbies and activities that give you joy, practice them.

Hiding the things that give you joy, ultimately means hiding significant parts of yourself.

Think more about how you see yourself than how others see you. Get used to adopting your vision and not being obsessed with other people's points of view. Most of the negative thoughts you may have about yourself originate from how you think others see you.

Another important aspect from which many women find the benefit is learning to be merciful to yourself. You're not a robot; you're not a machine. Don't always make the best or the right decisions.
Reason in the terms that you have decided in the past, the choices you have made, and maybe today you think they were wrong, in reality, they were not. Even if they have caused you pain and sorrow.
The truth is that back then, at that moment, you needed to make that choice.
Let me explain better: in that "past", that is to say in that context, and in that situation, what you could have chosen was what life had better to offer you, and that you considered right. So, if you did that, it's because you precisely needed that particular thing at that time, or you needed to live that specific situation.
What life put you through and what you grabbed was the best that life had to offer you. It was the right decision for you.
Start thinking that life has always offered you the best, and it will continue to do so. If you don't think it's the best, the best ain't going to happen.

Being yourself is not a difficult task, but becoming aware of yourself can take time and effort. It takes courage to show yourself to the world, knowing that not everyone will like you. It takes the "shamelessness" to set high standards. Getting closer to yourself, to your true self, is a path, but never an effort; otherwise, it means that you have not been honest with yourself about your needs and desires.

This book also talks about finally making peace with the person you are, even if not everyone will accept you. The inability of someone to take you as you are does not diminish your value at all.
You will never be happy if you are not yourself to the end. So,

as hard as it is, you have to take the risk.

Go out into the world and show your uniqueness. You, your dignity, your trust, your happiness, are worth the risk. Give yourself the best gift ever - love for yourself - and allow yourself to become the person you always wanted to be, but never allowed to exist.

Conclusion

This book intended to enhance your uniqueness as a woman, and to make you feel at the height of all those situations you encounter in life. Furthermore, I wanted to give you the knowledge to know who you are, and to provide you with the possibility to be fully yourself. But above all, to avoid becoming the person that others want you to be.

In the initial chapters, you have understood the importance of really finding out who you are, to best express the characteristics that make up your uniqueness. It is what must give you the strength to come out into the open to dig and understand how you really are. And it's also the reason why you don't have to be afraid to be yourself and to want to value yourself. You deserve it! That's the meaning of your purpose; that's your why.

It's important not to be influenced or conditioned, to do that. Above all, do not be afraid of it.

The factors that primarily affect you are family, friends, and the education we have received. When you decide to evolve, it is fundamental to be aware that these can be dangerous. That's when it becomes necessary to be strong enough to resist these external stimuli; first of all, those coming from the people closest to you are the ones that can affect you the most.

The next step is to valorize yourself, to feel, and to convince yourself that you deserve more, and you can only do this by setting higher standards. It also helps to increase self-esteem and self-confidence. With this, you also understand that it is all alone and only in your hands. You decide how you want to live, the steps you want to take, and the goals you want to achieve. And in this case, you have to rely only on yourself; you cannot rely on other factors.

In this path of personal growth, for a woman, it is more necessary than ever to understand that not everyone can accept it, and on the other hand, it is not even needed. When you have the security of your means and your abilities, this aspect takes a back seat.

If you want to succeed, you have to do the opposite of what people think and do. To stand out is what leads you on a profitable path, where the great mass is not present. And it is on this terrain that you find the most significant opportunities, not only for growth.

Changing the perspective of seeing things, the world, and reality, puts you in a position to evolve and achieve what you want. This aspect goes hand in hand with another "evolution" that you should make, which is to change some habits and limiting mental paradigms. Why do this? As you have seen, it is precisely the factors that generally prevent you from achieving success.

Becoming aware of yourself, and growing from your person, also implies knowing how to manage the unpleasant and uncomfortable feelings and moods that you go through during the phases of life.

Equally important is not judging, to which an entire chapter has been dedicated because it is a limiting habit common among people. Judging others is what attracts us to the judgments of others.

Judging makes you live in a low vibrational state, which is precisely the opposite of what you need to grow and prosper as a person. The opposite is crucial, however, to be in a state of positive vibrations, because this is the only way you can attract the positive energy, on which so many things depend.

Finally, to become aware of how vital it is to be yourself to the end and live according to your values, which are not necessarily those you carry with you from childhood or that you have been taught, is what gives you the strength to do so. To discover your true self, allow it to prosper, and follow it all your life. You deserve changes that will lead you to benefits. So, prepare to achieve success in the field of your choice, as if you have already completed it. Believe it, and prepare your mind and your body for novelty and change.

The next step is to put into practice what you have learned from these pages because theory must be followed by action.
Self-discovery and personal transformation are not easy, so do not let yourself be discouraged.
Aim to make the changes most completely and serenely possible. You only have to gain from them. Rushing to face them will not help you.
Happiness depends on making concrete steps forward. Now that you have the information you need to find out who you are, it is essential to use it in everyday life, as well as in the specific circumstances you will encounter.

Reviews are an author's sap, whatever genre he writes. They allow him to continue writing more helpful books. Without stars and reviews, you would never have found this book. If you would click five stars on your Kindle device, that will ensure that I can continue to produce again, and I sincerely appreciate it.

Please take just twenty seconds of your time to support an independent author by leaving a review on the platform where you purchased this book.

Thank You!

Sincerely,

Jay K. Morley

As a way of saying thanks for purchasing this book, there is a gift for you. A more topical issue than ever. Find out how to avoid falling into sneaky fear traps and stay healthy.

Simply copy and paste the link below into your browser, to get your gift:

https://dl.bookfunNEL.COM/61q2slgkvy

Also available from Jay K. Morley:

- The Transformation You Can. Your Personal Guide to the Seven Simple and Basic Rules to Wisdom and Change.

- Change the Days of Your Life. The Personal Guide You Should Read

- Getting Your Life Back: How to Demystify Your Beliefs and Meet Your Authentic Self

- Let Love Shape Your Life. The Way to Your New Self

- The Law of Attraction Secrets You Wish You Knew. How and For Whom It Works

CPSIA information can be obtained
at www.ICGtesting.com
Printed in the USA
BVHW040952121120
593172BV00016B/1824